T0118372

For anyone who has felt the joys and sorrows of unconditional love. These poems uniquely describe what so many feel, yet may have a hard time putting into words.

Somethin's in My Water

Somethin's in my water
I never felt like this before
What else could cause such joy?
It's affecting my concentration.
Got to be an outside stimulation
Somethin', must be in my water

I am not one to complain
What could be causing this pain?
It's bittersweet; what could it be
Call a doctor! Get me a remedy
Somethin' is in my water!
Perchance it is not true
I surmise it is you

Sherry A. Wright

iUniverse, Inc.
New York Bloomington

Somethin's in My Water

iUniverse books may be ordered through booksellers or by contacting:

iUniverse
1663 Liberty Drive
Bloomington, IN 47403
www.iuniverse.com
1-800-Authors (1-800-288-4677)

ISBN: 978-1-4401-2952-0 (pbk)
ISBN: 978-1-4401-2953-7 (ebk)

Printed in the United States of America

iUniverse rev. date: 3/24/2009

ACKNOWLEDGMENTS

The writing of "Somethin's in My Water" comes from love. It was not an easy task putting emotions into words. I let the words find me. I could not have reached so deeply to bring this book to fruition without the blessings and support of certain individuals.

First, I thank God for His blessings to write this book. God laid this book on my heart and blessed me with special people to awaken my spirit.

Secondly, I thank Londel O'Neal the seed and foundation of "Somethin's in My Water". I thank Londel for his inspiration and encouragement. Thanks to Londel the words and the ingredients to what I call "Inspiredwordsoul" no longer are stuck in the chambers of my heart or lay dormant at the bottom of my soul. He has been a positive and encouraging influence.

I thank Lovell J. Wright. Although Lovell was not aware I was writing this book, he has been a motivating influence. Lovell is indeed the wind beneath my wings.

Thanks and much appreciation to.

Ivy and Gwen Williams- For their tell it like it is-ness
Debbie Sparks- The book doctor for encouragement and proofing
Tim Dodd- First to buy my first book and an amiable co-worker
Honorable Hal and Mary Daub- For leadership and motivation
Birdie Christianson- For all the positive feed back and enthusiasm
Ramona Cano- For listening and sharing

Inspiredwordsoul for your support and friendship

Shatavia Peoples-Brown
Gearldine Peoples
Carl Bertch
Angie Deck-Wright

To Lonnie

No man can close a door God has opened

You are the tree

You are the breeze

Contents

100 REASONS I AM GLAD YOU ARE IN MY LIFE

1. *You are my friend*
2. *You inspire me*
3. *You greet me with a smile*
4. *The destination is not important it is our journey*
5. *I want to reveal to you, what I have not to the world*
6. *You bring out the resourcefulness in me*
7. *You've awaken something inside of me*
8. *You gave me something I did not know was missing*
9. *Your presence made me aware*
10. *You were angry, got over it and did not mention it again*
11. *You give me eye to eye moments*
12. *You are enigmatic at interval*
13. *You never tell me "I can't"*
14. *Because you hear me*
15. *You allow me to stare*
16. *You said you had my back*
17. *You said "The sky is the limit"*
18. *You said we see eye to eye*
19. *You accept my sometimes craziness*
20. *You kept me from falling*
21. *You take my breath away*
22. *You encourage me*
23. *You bring out the me in me*
24. *You empower me*
25. *You stir my emotion*
26. *You bring out the love in me*
27. *You make my day*
28. *You have not tried to fix me*

29. *You get me to think*
30. *You stimulate me*
31. *Because of who you are now*
32. *You touch my heart*
33. *We can be silent*
34. *We can be in the moment*
35. *You say the things I want to hear*
36. *You seem to read my mind*
37. *You enhance my imagination*
38. *You are telepathic (we do not need words to communicate)*
39. *You brighten my day*
40. *You have handled my heart with care*
41. *You have resolve*
42. *Your touch is strong, yet gentle*
43. *I look at you and see me*
44. *You are patient*
45. *You are interesting*
46. *You are smart*
47. *The way you produce results*
48. *Knowledge and growth*
49. *Your sensitivity*
50. *You make an effort*
51. *You are the tree*
52. *You are the breeze*
53. *I trust you*
54. *The conflict and confusion helps me grow*
55. *I like it when you are spontaneous*
56. *Our relationship may change…It will not end*
57. *Because you're here and now*
58. *I trust you will handle with care*
59. *I know you are in my life for a reason*

60. *You got whip appeal*
61. *Because you are you*
62. *You're unique*
63. *When you are near I have thermite moments*
64. *It is hard not to*
65. *I can't help myself*
66. *You always say the right thing at the right time*
67. *It was meant to be*
68. *There is always a reason*
69. *You challenge me*
70. *You give me freedom*
71. *When we are spontaneous and in the moment*
72. *How you look in your clothes*
73. *How your clothes look on you*
74. *The way you move*
75. *The way you "be" in your element*
76. *The way you walk*
77. *The way you talk*
78. *The way you breathe*
79. *The way you sleep*
80. *The way you think*
81. *The way we argue*
82. *The way we make up*
83. *The way you communicate*
84. *The way you maneuver*
85. *Because of where you have been*
86. *Because of your total-ness*
87. *You're there when I need you to be*
88. *Every day I find more reason to love you*
89. *The way you do the things you do*
90. *Just because*

Chapter 1
Acknowledging Love

Acknowledging Love

I have come prepared, with 100% heart, 100% soul, produced exclusively for you. There are some things you need to understand. If you find imperfections, they are not defects or flaws. More significantly they do not diminish my value. So please note, what you may perceive as blemishes are natural characteristics of life experiences and reflects the quality works created with God's very own hands adding the qualities of passion, love and empathy to complete my totalness. He made my inner fabric with beauty and endurance. He gave my soul a heart to balance the conflicts of the mind. Together they formed a bond of love patiently strong, respectfully bold and forever blessed. A love the mind could never conceive or possess.

My garment is an earthly covering for my heart and soul, a protection of sort. It is there for those who cannot see past my garment to the depth and the degrees of my being; unlike you who can touch my heart and arouse my soul. I am a special and unique product. I have passed a heavenly inspection. I am a classic product, registered and trademarked by God Himself; One of a kind, authentic premium being. I am the result of the collaboration of thousands of passionate and creative angels with the management and seal of God.

Although I am impact resistance, I am an incomplete product and my fabric is more body than image. I may have a tendency to flourish when exposed directly to society's impositions. I have the courage, strength and conviction to filter out any and all critics in order to maintain. Therefore every precaution should be taken in order to avoid exposures. God the manufacturer and I the distributor are not responsible for society's labels related to the above conditions. I do not exist as a result of other perceptions or deceptions for their perceptions are their reality, not my reality. They do not decide my value. This woman's heart and soul are not licensed or leased to any person or installation. I have a sense of humor about everything and take great pride in myself. I decide my value.

Caution and Care Instructions:

I carry no tags or labels for they are a deterrent to growth. The process is the most advanced available and the uniqueness is created and manufactured for me and sent directly to you for support, laughter and love. To maintain confidence and perfect blend always use the gentle cycling of respect and provide ample room for every necessity and freedom of movement and you will always receive the maximum return in consistency, quality and honesty. In accordance with the Surgeon General, there is no risk of impairment, contamination or ailment to your mental or physical health. When treated with respect and compassion you can be assured our friendship will endure.

All My Life (I have been waiting for you)

I have been waiting for you
Maybe, just maybe, it's not you,
The way you walk is how he would walk
And, you talk the way he'd talk
The way you stir up my emotions
I did not know it would be like this
My mind, my heart in such a commotion
I've been waiting…
All my life

When I think of you
My heart skips a beat, the way he'd make it do
And, oh, the way you bring on that whip appeal
Makes me feel the way he'd make me feel
Something is causing my heart to soar
Is it you I have been waiting for?
Cause' I have been waiting…
All my life

Cause' you do the things only he would do
Incessantly, I am thinking of you
You say the things he would say
My life has changed since you've come my way
You challenge me to wonder and explore
Could you be the one I am waiting for?
I have been waiting
All … my life

I'll allow him to know me
And, he'll love me unconditionally
Perhaps you are here to help me grow
For when he comes, I will know
So long, I have waited for this day
Someone like you to come my way
I ... have been...waiting
All my life

You say what he'd say
You talk like he'd talk
You are everything now, he will be
What is it that I cannot see?
If you are real,
Why am I waiting still?
All my life... All my life
I have been waiting for you
All my life

If You are Thankful for the Love Be Thankful for the Pain

I can listen to the Blues all night
The low down, down home blues
Singing of love gone wrong, getting it right
Trying to make it understood
That love can hurt so good
Who would believe there is good in pain?
Pain of love... Pain of passion...
It is all the same,
Pain too soon forgotten
You thanked God for the love you found
You have to thank Him for the pain
That got you feeling down

I get my joy when I think of you
The time with you was pleasure to
For a moment there, it was hard to maintain
Conceding that I cared, relieved the pain
There are no tears even in grief
It happened; a smile is my relief
Love set free, it does not cease
It only changes in form and intensity
Your words, long after they are said
Still, in my head remain
I thank God; I know there's a reasons and
Purpose for the love...
And the pain

Please Understand

I love and care, Please understand
I appreciate the things you say and do
And, I hope all your dreams come true.
You are in my life because I need you to be
Sitting in silence, a smile or a glance
Enhances something in side of me
It may have happened a year ago or just yesterday
You have managed to touch my life in so many ways.

I want to wake up and see you there.
I want you to understand
I don't have to be the one with whom you share.
I can love you from anywhere.
It is not about who you choose;
It is about you, so there is no way I can lose
You can play me as if I were a toy;
Just be upfront, I'll only love you more.

Thoughts of you bring tears to my eyes
I want you to understand
It's not because I am feeling bad
My heart is smiling. I am not feeling sad
Tears and laughter are enthusiastic heartfelt explosions;
It is a chain reaction of my heart's emotions.

When I see you sitting there, I can only stare
I want you to understand
I'm inhaling and exhaling you to the depths of my soul
Wondering where you begin and where you end
So very glad you are my friend.
My laughter is really an oversized smile.
Conflicts and differences aside,
I hope this friendship will last awhile

I use the word love, Please understand,
That it is I who do not comprehend,
The games you play
The charms you display
The sound of your voice
I do believe I have a choice
I love you and I care
I just want you to understand

I Only Love You When

I only love you when
You come into view
And everytime I think of you
With each breath I take
Before I go to sleep … when I awake
I only love you when
You sit, stand or walk
And everytime I hear you talk
In everyway
Each God given moment…each God given day

I only love you when
I see the trees dance with the breeze
When I open or close my eyes
Every sunset … every sunrise

I only love you when
My heart beats
When I'm hungry, when I eat
When I hear the music
Of a bird, the wind … a sweet melody

I only love you when
I count my blessings
When I write
In the middle of the night
When I lay me down to sleep
And pray the Lord … our love to keep

Stranded On The Other Side Of Love

I open my heart with a commitment to maintain
The love is overflowing and hard to restrain
My heart lie silent, as a snow flake
Floating to the ground
And I am found …
Stranded, on the other side of love

My emotions are off the chart
Anxious to find directions for my heart
It dips and dives, and scurries,
Resembling, a fallen leaf crossing the road
Going up, going down while
Stranded on the other side of love

At the end of the day
When you turn and go your way
I am filled with passion,
excited with every thought
Yet, I stand … I stand
Stranded on the other side of love

With only a glimpse of the emotions of love
I sit and stare
In reach, unable to share
I can smell it, feel it, taste it
Stranded, on the otherside of love

You need to recognize
You've awaken that special place
Where my love resides
Awake ... conscious … aware and
Stranded … on the other side of love

The Only Gift

Santa checked his list. He checked it twice
I have been both naughty and nice
There is only one gift I want under my Christmas tree
It is not going to come down my chimney
I can imagine my gift on Santa's sleigh
Being delivered on Christmas Day

There is only one gift I want this year
It's a gift that will bring me Holiday cheer
Unwrapping gifts is so much fun
My Christmas list is a list of one
The only gift to make my wish come true
The only Christmas gift I want to unwrap
... Is you

More Than a Holiday

When we count our blessings
Our Christmas will be merry and bright

The New Year will bring you blessings
And every night will be Silent Night Holy Night

TURN YOUR LOVE ON (I WISH IT WERE ME)

I know if you ever love,
It would be a love so true
That's what I see in you
An immeasurable love … And I wish it were me

I can tell if you ever love,
You'd fulfill every necessity
A Heaven made love, only you can achieve
I see it … And I wish it were me

If you ever turned your love on
You'd set someone's love on fire
You'd be their hearts desire
I know, I can tell, I can feel it
Ooh, I wish it were me

If you ever love
I know you'll be right there
Always ready, not hesitating to share
You possess the power and passion to
Your every heart beat, will beat for two
I wish it would beat for me

You'd be my world if you ever loved me
Be my partner, my lover, my friend
There would be no reason to pretend
When I awake from this dream
I'll still wish it were me

When I examine the love in me
You're the only one I see
Every time I see you standing there
My love I want to share
Someone to give my love to
And I wish it were you

I know if you ever turned your love on
You'd hold on real tight
You'd try to make every thing all right
You'd be the tree, you'd be the breeze
Ooh gee, I wish it were me
I wish … it were … me

Really!

Need you ask, if I love you or if I care?

As much if not more than men need air

When I love, I admit, it's more about me than you

It is not about what you can do for me

It is what I can do for you

Like, what can I do to make it a better day?

Maybe it comes from the heart…the soul?

No one really knows

Could be a scientific thing

like our genes or DNA

caused by chemicals in my brain

My brain is smarter than me, really!

I wish I could make it clear so you will understand

No expectations, no demands

I hope you find happiness in every thing you get

and anyone you are with

It is not so much about me as for me

Because it makes me happy;

Liking you ... caring about you

It feels good too, really!

I don't know if I'll ever wish anyone love again

It hurts, really!

It hurts when there is no direction,

when it is ignored and when it is denied

I really wish you understood

I can't quite grasp it myself;

Why you? Why not you?

We will never be on the same page
There will always be differences in opinions
Other wise we will be giving up ourselves,
sacrificing our individual values and beliefs
We can agree to disagree, really!

A person should know they are loved by
someone in the universe
It will never be my intent to hurt
harm, offend or disrespect you
I know, you know my heart
Once I love, it cannot be taken back
It may change in direction, degrees or depth
I know me; I can only give love that last forever
Really!

A Letter

It only took a second
To write this letter
Actually it was written the day we met
I had not known it yet
I did not know it then
How, where or when did it begin?

It only took a moment it did not take long
To write you this song
How, where or when did it all begin?
I can hear the music now as I did then
The melody was very clear
You entered my heart, right here

That is why it only took a moment
To say this prayer for you
Please and thank you
The strongest prayer I know
May you find happiness in all you do
And wherever you go

There may come a time
I may never see you again
So, I'll write a letter, sing you a song
Only God knows, this is where you belong
He knows I care and find it hard to convey
To show you I care; I write, I sing, I pray

WHEN CAN I STOP LOVING YOU?

You are on my mind when I go to bed
Before I open my eyes, thoughts of you enter my head.
I ask myself, when, can I stop loving you?
When the sky is green and the grass is blue
Then I can stop loving you
When the moon no longer lights the night
And the stars stop shining so bright
When hurricanes are only a breeze
And, tornadoes are no more than a sneeze
When raindrops are dry
And clouds stand still in the sky
When birds no longer sing in the trees
And the sweetness of flowers no longer attract the bees.
When there is no need for time
And all "mankind" is just "one kind"
When men can fly and cars are obsolete
And passengers can buy round trip tickets to eternity
When the doors to Heaven open for public tours
And choir voices are angelically pure
When all men live by faith and not by sight
And no one cares who is wrong or right
When war is only historical
And, Peace is eternal
Then, I can stop loving you

One Kiss One Hug

I don't want to kiss and say goodbye,
It would be too hard and only make me cry.
I don't want one last hug or one last time
Could not bear to feel your body next to mine.
A simple kiss or a gentle squeeze would be too much,
To walk away after your tempting touch.
I don't want to look into your eyes
Knowing, I would be instantly immobilized.
Each time your energy enters the room… and it is not a notion
My mind, body and soul become a whirlwind of emotion
I don't want to hear, "Let's talk" or "Baby let's take a walk".
Cause' every time I hear your voice
I lose my power to make a choice.
I love you, and this you must understand
There are no exceptions and no demands.
Just want you to be happy and to be free
To choose whatever you want to do or be.
I am not going to hope and wish for you to be mine
That would be a waste of time.
Cause' either you won't or either you will.
My only requirement is for you to be real.
I don't need promises, contracts or guarantees
It means we're not where I want us to be.
There is only one thing I need
And that is to share the love that's inside of me
With one kiss, one hug, one time
Lasting a lifetime

Birthday Wish and a Prayer

With all the written words in books, poems and songs
None can express or explain
Even my words, sometimes, don't come out right
So, the only thing for me to do...
Is... maintain
Tried the internet, and I could not find
A birthday song worthy of a friend of mine
I wanted it to be real
I wanted it to be true
Because this friend is special
This friend is you
Spent hours at Hallmark, it was not meant to be
Finding words, expressing how much you mean to me
So, to show you how much I care
I'm sending you these words along
With a wish and a prayer

The Wish:
If I were a Genie, I'd grant your every wish
And you'd have all your needs supplied
No wish or prayer would ever be denied
My wish is for whatever you need or desire
I wish you love, health and peace; whatever
Sets your soul afire

The Prayer:
I pray for wisdom and patience to be a good friend
Understanding that some days you're the tree
Some days you're the breeze
I pray these words enhance your Birthday
And brings a smile your way
Words are not necessary to show I care
That's why I am sending you
A wish and a prayer

You Said You Said

You said. You Said. You said.

You said you thought we saw eye to eye

You said the sky is the limit

You said you had my back

Tell me, tell me.

How come I don't feel all that?

You said you said you said

You said you don't lie

You said you were for real

All I know is - You've got skills

You said, you said, you said

You said I did not have to wait

You said you were my friend

Next thing I know you frontin'

No need to pretend

Now let's move on to chapter 2

You asked if I trusted you

Yes, yes I do

You asked if I believed you'd be

Upfront, tell it like it is

You even asked if I loved you

I hesitated, made some excuse

But you know, you know I do

Now I'm asking you to believe me

When I say I do, I do, I do

You say the right things I like to hear

Your timing is just right

I try to resist with all my might

There's nothing I can do, nothing I can say
So, I just walk away
I did not choose love, love chose me
If love is a choice, who, would choose such pain?
"Eye to eye", "what is yours is mine", "got my back!"
No, I am not from Missouri
Still, I need to know where you at!?

You are I and I am You

I can't complain or criticize
Because I am you and you are I
To get angry at you
I'd have to be angry at myself to
You say what I want to say
You must be reading my mind
When I am searching for answers
Your answers are right on time

If I am patient and wait
You'll tell me what I want to know
And when you are ready
You'll tell me when it is time to go
From the beginning, I could tell
Your spirit is burned into my soul
Your soul, carved into my heart
You are I and I am you
It has been that way from the start

There You Are

No matter where or when, you were always there
You have been there every minute of every day
I ran up the stairs and down again. You were not there
I looked around; I could not find you anywhere
I ran down the road. Where are you?
I looked at the clock it was 3 in the morning
I began to get concerned
I sat down and closed my eyes
In the dark I searched and searched and searched
You had been there so many times

I opened my eyes, looked over my shoulder
I have always wanted you there
I know you are here somewhere
You have always been there so many times before
From the moment my heart opened its' doors
The power of love was too much for me
Sensations too intense, I wanted to be free
The awareness of you invaded my mind
I thought of you all the time

I surveyed my mind, every cell.
Searched every lobe, every detail
Placed my hand over my heart and I began to smile
Hear that beat, ca thump, Ca thump?
There you are; you haven't gone far
It was only a moment; it seemed like an eternity
I found you here
Here, in my heart

Love without Interference

He does not hurry, yet he completes everything on time
I do not asks, yet he supplies all I need
He does not demand
He does not force, yet the right thing is said
He does not persuade

He forgives, no storm can last forever
Every storm has its blessings
He ask, and he receives
He knocks and my door is open

He gives by hearing
He loves by understanding
To give and to receive are a gift of love
He is …and I believe
Love without interference

Love Chooses You

If love is a choice, who would choose such pain
Who would go through that over and over again?
You don't choose love, love chooses you
It does not knock on your door, it comes from within
You open your heart, that's when it begins
You can't step back
You let love in, now, you have no choice
You do not choose love
Love chooses you

Chapter 2
Inspiredwordsoul

INSPIREDWORDSOUL RECIPE

Often we cannot find the words to convey or express to those we love and care about. With the inspiration of others, I've reached and came up with my own recipe for Inspiredwordsoul

Preparation:

Mix a bulk of "Believe"

with a pack of conceive.

Patience:

Slowly simmer, Inspirewordsoul takes time.

Hearing:

Listen to your heart blended with soul,

after separating from the mind.

Seeing:

Flavor with enthusiasm and visualize the process.

Breathing:

Inhale life's positive and exhale your creativeness.

If done correctly, you'll begin to smile.

Now let it marinade for awhile

Season with love and stir in the passion

Sprinkle in stimulating imagination

Take pen in hand, a multitude of

Inspiredwordsoul will unfold

After all, how much love can a heart hold?

So Happy You Had a Birth-Day (There is a wish)

There are no cards or words
To convey or express
My hopes and thoughts for your birthday happiness
There are no gifts I can make or buy you
That is greater than those God has placed inside you
There is a wish I can make for sure
My wish …
That your Birthday celebration is all
You wished for.
Your Birth—Day
Gives me reason to celebrate everyday!

God the Comedian

Out of the Blue

He sent me you.

Thought I was drunk

Out of my mind.

Something is in my water,

Cause I do not drink wine.

What is the deal?

Is this for real?

I tried to pretend.

Told my heart "Don't let him in".

Before I had a chance

For any romance;

My heart broke.

This must be a joke.

What is the punch line?

God … You messin' with my mind?

God, you're trying to be funny?

Now! … You send me a honey?

You are very amusing.

The Comedian, doing His thing.

I Thought,
"On my way to the funny farm."
I know He meant no harm.
I have a sense of humor too.
I see what God is trying to do.
He has a plan and a purpose,
I should have waited a while
Because, you do make me smile.
God really pulled one on me.
Thank you God for being so funny.

Today I Saw You Smile

You know, that's what I like—your smile
One, I have not seen in awhile
A ray from Heaven, right here on earth
Indeed, I have been blessed by your birth
So, you are going away, too soon—too far
Wherever you are, wherever you go,
You'll still be my shining star
The way you smile, the way you play
Goes down in history as my favorite days
Yes, today I saw you smile
And, I smiled too, inside and out
Cannot explain what that's all about
Today, I felt your smile
When you go away,
I'll think of you once in awhile
And ... my heart ... my soul ... will smile

God is an Artist

With God's creative skills he sculptured and
Transported you to earth.
He selected you from His sacred garden
And programmed your birth.
He allowed you to stumble and even fall.
You'll need help and He awaits your call.
He gave you challenges to make you aware.
He gave you only the pain you could bear.
Gradually you'd become the man you are.
Special, talented and smart, one of His best so far.
He knows your mind and your heart.
He's known your abilities from the start.
Perhaps, you have noticed you have been blessed.
His work is an ongoing process.
He not only created your outsides,
His most intricate work is deep within.
You're title free, clear of all liens; you're
Warranted from beginning to end.
God is an artist; His tool is love.
He accomplishes His work from above.
God's hands touched you with special care.
I know of no other that can compare.
God is a great artist, an original too
I know, I can see
His work, in you.

I vs. U ... A Spectator's Sport

It is not Broadway
It is not even a play
Check this ... News Flash! Report! Report!
We are not a Spectator's sport
It is a conversation between us two
There is constant observation, it is sad but true
We are not the NFL or the NBA
Why are they interested in what we say?
News Flash! Report! Report!
We are not a Spectator's sport
How they stare and listen for our every word
They watch in amazement and do not disturb
I, forget they are even there
Just you and me, I must declare.
News Flash! Report! Report!
No way, no how we are a Spectator's sport
What on earth are they watching for?
A move? A word? A confirmation?
Perhaps a chance to witness a revelation!

In A Moment

What if the years went by and you never knew
I really cared for you?
Why wait for Christmas, a Birthday
Or some man-made holiday.
Tomorrow is not promised for either of us
So, in the moment, I got serious.
I opened the gates to my eyes, ears and heart,
It only took a moment for you to slip in
I made a choice, knowing that I could
Never go back again
My defenses comes down
Whenever you come around.
It took sometime for me to reveal
All the feelings, I tried to conceal.
The gates are fully open, to my eyes and my heart too
There is still only room for you.
The gates to my ears opened and I heard a sound
Sounds of you in my head, I could not quiet them down.
All the gates leading to the rooms in my soul
Opened only a crack.
I hesitated a moment and it was too late
To push you back.
I know this may seem strange
The thoughts in my head, I must rearrange.
I don't understand, I just don't see
What is this Hocus Pocus you've put on me.

Not a Secret

It is not a secret that I cannot reveal
It is not something I want to conceal
It's private and personal between you and I
Feelings I refuse to justify.
They are not secrets, but thoughts I am
Unwilling to share
With those that will judge and compare
Not interested in others perceptions
When it comes to my undisclosed conceptions
It's not a secret, from my point of view
It's not a mystery to look into
Its laughter, love and heartfelt treasures
It's about friendship and all its' pleasures
It's the stimulation I want to keep secure
From those that turn truth into rumor
This is information I can't wait to share
With someone, with my words, will take care
There are feelings I try not to show
They're in a place; I'll only allow you to go.
There are no secrets, no illusions
You have the key to clear up any confusion

I Am Not Afraid of You Anymore

Afraid, of you? Not anymore
Wanting to see you ... Take a glance
Afraid to see you, didn't want to take that chance
Checking to see if you're here or there
Had mixed and weird feelings from who knows where
I am not afraid of you anymore
Afraid, of you? Not anymore
I was afraid of what I could not see
Afraid of all the feelings inside of me
Couldn't figure out my reactions
Finally had to admit, there is an attraction.
It was not the packaging or the physical view
What attracted me, is inside of you
Did not want to be rude
So, I stood back, not to intrude
I tried to figure out your nonverbal clues
Conflicting and confusing, you know it's true
Had to learn how to communicate
It took some trials, now we can relate
Afraid? ... Of you? ... Of me? ... Not anymore.

LOVE

Caress it!

Breathe it!

Honor it!

Defend it!

Respect it!

Enjoy it!

Accept it!

Share it!

Behold it!

Admire it!

Console it!

Free it!

Enhance it!

Remember it!

Sense it!

Soothe it!

Inhale it!

Exhale it!

Believe it!

LOVE!

Just DO It!

Thank God for It!

The Hardest Part

The hardest part
Is not the beginning
Is not the ending
The hardest part
Is not the fight
Not who's wrong or right
The hardest part is
Unable to touch
And loving too much
The hardest part is
The intense desire
A soul on fire
The hardest part is
Being near
And the relationship is not clear
The hardest part is
The words I cannot convey
When the tears of pleasure come my way
The hardest part is
When you come to me
And surges of joy are overwhelmingly
The hardest parts are …
Not only the hardest
They are the best

May I Have This Dance?

So glad we met, please don't go
May I have this dance, nice and slow?
A step to the right, feel that beat
A glide to the left, I am feeling the heat
A slight tilt to the back, in the groove
A smooth step forward, I love the way you move
My arms, one around your waist the other
On your back
It's getting hard to breathe … Heart attack!
I'm having a thermite moment with your perfect grip
Placed just right to make that dip
Floating, body to body, cheek to cheek
The mood in here is getting deep
Is it the music or is it me?
Please don't let go, don't set me free
Forget the music, let's just stand here and sway
Knowing when the music stops, you'll walk away
I'm glad I took a chance
To ask you for this slow dance
How about another one
You make it so much fun!

Spiderman

Spiderman, Spiderman where You at?
Come into your parlor? I'm not going for that.
Spiderman, Spiderman, Don't want to fall prey
I am spellbound, can't go away
I call you Spiderman, not to be offensive
A woman around you, has to be defensive
Spiderman, Spiderman, I'm well aware
May not be so bad to be caught up in your snare
Spiderman, Spiderman, where you at?
Tempted to enter your parlor ... I'm not going for that!
I don't see you as a pest
I'll come a little closer to tell you the rest
You're strong, cunning and smart too
That's why I have great respect for you
Spiderman, Spiderman, you're downright clever
If I get to close, I'll be gone forever
You're quick, skillful and nice
I've seen your web; don't want to pay the price
I'm not going to be your fly
I don't need me to tell you why

Till You Use Me Up

Use me, till you use me up

Here's your chance to rise to the occasion

Don't need to play me, I need no persuasion

Use me till you use me up

Do it now … In style

Not in a little while

Don't put me away

To be used someday

I must admit, I'm glad you're here

I know, you know, I have no fear

Don't set me aside

Just to build your pride

Use me, till you use me up

Go ahead, please proceed

Take whatever you need

No need to play me like a puppet

What you want, you got it

You can use me till you use me up

Don't forget

And there'll be no regrets

Don't mistake, my kindness for weakness

Abuse me and you know what!

You gonna miss this!

TODAY'S CHALLENGES ARE TOMORROWS' BLESSINGS

You came into my life, the purpose or reason,
I know not why
God laid you on my heart, as time went by
I concluded, God has sent me a friend
Then, in a moment, out of the blue, conflict and
Confusion set in
I didn't understand, pressure began to take its toll
Too heavy was my heart, too transparent was my soul
I knew there was a purpose, but, the pain I could not bear
So I went to God, on my knees in prayer
I could not ask Him to take, you, His blessing away
I thanked God for the challenge he brought me today
I prayed for wisdom, so I could understand
Let go, let God, placed my needs in His hands
My load was lessened, yet remains
God's blessing sometime, comes with pain
He put you here to fulfill a need
I prayed for patience to let His plan succeed
I thank God for challenges every day
And for you, a blessings
He sent my way

Thoughts, Dreams and Imagination

Somewhat amazing, somewhat a thrill
Let's say borderline … surreal
Does not matter if I'm here or there
Does anyone even care?
It's my creation
An overactive imagination
Relationships are like a rocking chair
Rocking, Rocking, going nowhere
Fun filled thoughts, just fantasy
Someone up there, playing a joke on me
Thoughts, dreams, imagination, once conceived
Becomes real, yet hard to believe
Appears I have heart constipation
Need to buy a ticket, send my mind on vacation
Have I gone to extreme?
After all, it's only a dream

Undoubtedly, it's been a thrill
Don't need a straight jacket; I know it's not real
Just blood pumpin' … Pulse jumpin'
Hands perspire … Soul afire
Heart smiling … Body trembling
What the mind conceives
The body believes
Thoughts, dreams and imagination
Like an Oscar winning movie, except it is free
Who am I kidding?
You are real and forever a part of me

I Apologize

No need
To justify
Nothing to rectify
Be kind
Be blind
To words once said
Now dead
Gentle Touch
Too much
It's a new day
New way
Not about winning
New beginning
Reflect
Respect
Don't say it
Pray it
Convey it
No need to conversate
To relate
No stress
Confess
Express
Forgiveness
Be wise
Compromise
I Apologize

Can I Please Sneak a Peek?

Can I please sneak a peek?
Because I like you and I care
If you need me, I will be there
I don't blame you … It is a matter of trust
If it is not for me to know, keep your secrets, if you must.
Just give me a little peek
To what you like to do and what is it you'd like to say
Can I help you in any…way?
I know you're smart and well aware
There are no others that compare
You love and care about someone
What else motivates you? What is … your 911?
Give me a peek won't you please?
Tell me what you want and what you need
Give me just one little lead
Whatever it is … And you can believe
I am here unconditionally
I respect and I understand your privacy
Because, I too, have a place,
I'll only allow you to see
Can I Please … sneak a peek?

YOU

You devastate

I procrastinate

You inspire

I perspire

You touch my heart

I fall apart

You smile

I grin awhile

You move

I groove

You lighten up

I tighten up

You stimulate

I hesitate

You conversate

I relate

You get serious

I get delirious

You aggravate

I agitate

You explain

I complain

You play the game

I maintain

When You Are Not Here

Out-of-town or in another place,
In the same room, yet in another space.
You, I can no longer see or touch
And, I miss you a little too much.
A part of you … It remains clear
I will remember and you will be here.
You have left a mark of who you are
On who I am today.
I can recall you back to my mind and
Heart, even though you are faraway.
If we ever meet or never meet again
I will remember and be your friend.
I can still feel and hear your voice
When you are not here, I have no choice,
Rather it be times or miles
I will remember you and your smile.
As long as I remember … You
You … will always be here!

Come Inside

Come on, come in.
I'm glad you decided to be my friend.
Are you sure you'd like to come inside?
It's warm … comfortable, I have nothing to hide.
Come on, We will have lots to do.
I've made some plans, just for you.
Let's get to know each other, get in the zone.
We won't be interrupted, I'll disconnect the phone.
Now, I'll show you around; show you my treasures.
Go ahead enjoy, it's my pleasure.
There are some things I'd like you to know.
Of course, there are some places I'll only allow you to go
Would you like some food, some music?
Then you can show me your magic.
Got lots of games we can play
What's that? Abracadabra, you say?
You are really one of a kind.
Everything is going to work just fine.
I am a little nervous, not at all bold.
Let me get you some cover, are you cold?

Go ahead, get comfortable, and lay by the fire.
Let's talk, what's your desire?
I am so glad you came today.
Hope you can come again so we can play.
I've anticipated your visit for sometime.
Would've invited you sooner; I did not want to
Be out-of-line
Come on, it's going to be fun.
You know, you're a special someone.
Go ahead play your game.
When you are done, nothing will be the same.
I hope you enjoyed your visit, I had a ball!
I enjoyed your magic and all.
Thanks to you, I am inspired.
I am not at all tired.
I should give you a warning
Everything will be different, when you
Wake up in the morning.
… Goodnight

Love Is

Love Is:
No doubting
No judging
No fear
Love is here
Love is:
Accepting
Wanting
And Sharing
Love is Caring
Love is:
Devotion
Compassion
And affection
A heavy case of infatuation
Love brings:
Enjoyment
Enthusiasm
And Pleasure
You are the treasure
Love is:
Possible
Conceivable
Believable
Down right achievable

Love is you

Love is me

Love is always free

Love is!

Positive

Tender

Intense

If it's real, there is no pretense

A Piece of My Heart a Piece of My Soul

We became friends,
I felt it at the moment of conception.
I felt you, I felt the emotions.
Emotions, inside of me, so profound,
Were hard to contain
So intense … joy mixed with pain.
Right then, that moment in time
Thoughts of you filled my mind.
I know if I were to fall, your hands will be there,
To pick me up with gentle care.
I can only give you what I got.
Maybe you will want more, maybe not.
It is not a dream or my imagination
I feel you and I feel the emotion.
Even at this moment, words are hard to find.
Perhaps it is because; you are one of a kind.
You have taken a piece of my soul, a piece of my heart.
I feel it, here, here, and here, just like at the start.
Emotions, so profound the body finds them difficult to contain.
The feeling so intense, hard to maintain.
When it comes to problems, I'm an idealist
This friendship can cannot be destroyed or cease to exist
It can only change in quality and intensity
That's the way it was meant to be
As this friendship commence to unfold
I wonder … how much love …
Can this heart hold?

Chapter 3 Step on Back—Your Heart or Your Mind

Step on Back Collection Your Heart or Your Mind

We all feel the need sometimes in our lives to "step back". Step back and take another look at the person we are drawn to and/or ourselves. You have to make a choice to trust your heart or to listen to your mind. While your heart is being tugged and overflowing with emotions, you may not be aware of the hows and whys. Your mind is calling out to you society's values and opinions and technical aspects of relationships. The difference between a flower and a weed is only someone's perception; someone's opinion of how something should or should not be. Sometime "We thinketh too much". If we are to learn and grow we must try, fail and succeed. This is called growth. Love can only be experienced. Defining it is often conflicting, confusing and inaccurate. Explaining and defining love depends on the power of the mind, the openness of the heart and the depth of the soul; In other words your personal experience.

Therefore, this is where we step back. If need be, step way back. Laugh if you want to. Cry when you need to. Stepping back does not mean you are stepping away. It only hurts if the love is not acknowledge are set free. Failure does not exist. Again, it is someone's opinion how your relationship should be. Do not cry because it is over. Smile, because it happened. Use some "inspiredwordsoul", the energy of love. It cannot be destroyed, dissolved or cease to exist. Love, like a diamond, can only be changed in intensity or from one form to another. Step back and go for it. If it works use it, if it doesn't lose *it.*

Step on Back—It's Over

Whatever the reason, whatever the cause
It is time for us to take a pause
Step on back. It is over, it's true
No more me, no more you.
There doesn't have to be a reason.
We were not meant for a lifetime only a season.
I cannot explain it any other way.
It's been an experience, I must say
Inspired me and helped me to grow.
I am stepping on back, it's time to go.
There is nothing more we can share,
Yet, there is no other that can compare.
I remember the first time I saw you smile.
I know I am going to hurt awhile.
I will miss the laughter and the games.
I don't know how to extinguish these flames.
The fire still burns out-of-control.
I still feel you, deep in my soul.
I am not going to leave with, "We can be friends."
If you ever need me, I'll be here till the end.

I am going to love you whether you're here or not.
Just because you are gone, the love does not stop.
Step on back, away from me.
I don't want you to go and I don't want to be free.
I will be the first to concede,
If there is, ever, anything you need.
Step on back, your nearness is hard to bear.
I know, you know, I truly care.
For as much as it hurts to let you go;
It hurts more to love you so.
It will take all I have, not to reach and
Pull you back again.
So step on back and step back again.
Out of my reach, not out of my heart.
I care about you!
I told you that, from the start.

Step on Back—Before We Go There

Step back, for a moment before we go there.
Slow down, grab a chair
Think it out, don't make that move,
Even if you are in the groove.
The seasons vary and will change
It may, get a little strange
Perhaps I'm reading this all wrong
Can't ignore the vibes, cause' they are so strong.
I need, you need, we need … to step on back
Perplexed and bewildered, that's a fact
Right here, right now; just a touch
Needs, wants, desires; Are they ever too much?
It is the after that worries me
I fear my heart will never be free
Please step on back, got to catch my breath
I fear you are out of my depth
Step on back; don't think you want to go there
Let's wait, I'm here, I'm not going anywhere
What the soul wants: the mind fights
Yet, I know in my soul it will be all right
I just want to be fair

Are you sure we should go there?
Relationships, can be a strain
Just tell me the rules for this game.
Every word, every move; you amaze me!
I'm not stepping back, I must be crazy.
Step on Back
Are you sure?

I am willing and I am ready
I just cannot keep my knees steady
Come on, you want to go there?
Well I am right here, not going anywhere
Relationships can really get strained
I need to know if it is all fun and games
I'm not stepping back
I'm where I want to be, don't doubt it
Cause' Honey, I can't live without it

Step on Back—Get in Touch

You better step on back and get in touch
You just frontin' a little too much!
Step on back or go the other way
I'm not interested in what you got to say
I'm goin' to step forward, so ya gotta go
Step on back, you movin' too slow
It's been awhile, since you've talked to me
I'm cool with that, as you can see
You're just a little too close in my personal space
Step on back, get out of my face
You gotta stop trippin'
You going on and on about nothin'
Step on back, get in touch
Cause' Honey, you just frontin' a little too much
I'm gonna move on, you gotta get real
At this moment, you have no social appeal.
Step back, step on back
Your conversation is definitely getting whack
You're wasting my time
Just to give me a piece of your mind
Something you can't afford to lose
And I am getting a little confused
Step on back, step way back, I'm out of here.
Do me a favor and disappear

STEP ON BACK—STOP SNOOPIN'

You got to step on back and stop spying
You know I'm not lying
I see you peeping, coming around the corner creeping
You think I didn't notice you sitting over there
Why you watching me? What do you care?
I saw you walking behind, watching where I go
You thought I didn't know
I saw you listening who I talk to
I'm going to be me and do what I do
Are you someone's scout?
Step back, step on back, what is it all about?
Didn't realize I was so important
Glad I can provide you with some entertainment
Are you snooping for sport?
Or to give a report?
Step back, step on back.
Why you worried about what I do?
What I say and what I do, concerns me, not you.
I like to move, give out a shout.
It's not my problem you have nothing to dance about.
Come on step on back,

I'm not letting you bring me down.
Rumors and gossip, every time you come around.
Step back, step on back, and get a life.
Don't go bringing me your gripes
Step back, step on back, what, are you watching for?
Step on back and step back some more
Moving here, moving there, you are so obvious
I don't understand, why you are so curious
Perhaps you've learned a thing or two
Something I'm sure your mother taught you
What you're doing is out of place
Trying to intrude into others personal space
Step back, step on back.
Go have a good day
Hope you learned something
From what I had to say

Step on Back—Moment of Eternity

I promise you … this moment
I promise to express my feelings
As they are conceived
We only have this moment
It is, our eternity.
There is no tomorrow or yesterday
I am not stepping back
I am not going out that way.
We have no reason to forgive or apologize
There are no regrets, no reason to pretend
I love you this moment,
We are here, we are now.
There is no beginning, there is no end.
If there are obstacles, I see them as opportunities
To tell you, to show you, to experience you.
Each of my moments with you is an eternity.
Oh, no, I am not stepping back
I just can't go out like that.

If I think of yesterday or what tomorrow may bring
My feelings get mixed up with societal things.
Let's just be in the moment
Our moment, a moment of eternity.
I refuse to live my life by societal perceptions.
Society with its tunneled interpretations.
My soul, the world cannot touch or intimidate.
Because this moment is you, this moment is me.
Nothing and no one exist.
In this moment here, now,
Our moment of eternity
If you must go, that's the way it was meant to be.
I promise … I promise
My love for an eternity
I promise not to crush it, store it or hold it in
For another time until we can love again
There will be no stepping back
I will not, give up our moments like that
This is my moment, my life, and my love
I give it all to you … this moment
A moment of eternity

Step on Back—Where You Coming From?

Step Back, Step on back
Cause I don't know where you comin' from
So you want to play games—throw me a crumb
Oh, no! Honey you got to step on back
You ain't giving me no heart attack.
I like you and you like me.
Keep messin' around you'll be free.
Don't go telling me to get real.
When is the last time you told me how you feel.
It's not all your fault; I'll take some blame.
We both need to step on back, make a claim.
We only have now … this moment in time
For me to be yours and you to be mine.
If that's not the way you want it to be
Tell me, now, set my heart free.

Step on Back—You Know You Playing

I know you're playing, I know your game
Whatever you call it, it's all the same
It is BS and you know it
I'm telling you now, it is time to quit
Take it and spread it somewhere, anywhere
I'm telling you, I don't care
So step on back …. Step… on back

I am not interested, I told you before
If you are playing, don't knock on my door
You know my heart wants no other
We both play are we go no further
If you must spread your game, take it away from me
Gaming is not new; it's been around for centuries
Step on back…Step … on back…please

You better step back; grab a better point of view
This is getting redundant and you don't have a clue
You got game and you play it to win
There will be no sweepstakes won here my friend
Go ahead take your game and spread it if you so desire
In this place, this space, your play is not required
Step on back…step on back
Step … on back…..
Thank you

Step on Back—A Christmas Card Like This

I'm stepping on back to wish you a Merry Christmas
I'm stepping on back this Holiday season
You are very, very special, that's the only reason
I'm stepping back to get a better view
And to share something special with you
I'm stepping back from the shopping and wrapping
I'm giving you this card and a gift, only one of a kind
I know dear Santa will deliver it, right on time

This gift is meant just for you and it's not returnable
Don't even try it, it is not refundable
It comes unwrapped; it is free… yet priceless
You have so many God given talents and gifts
You can add these to the ones you already possess
And, it only comes… in a Christmas card like this

I'm stepping on back to wish you a Merry Christmas
I'm stepping back to wish you an enthusiastic Holiday
May your hopes, dreams and wishes all come your way
I wish it for a lifetime, not just this Holiday season
Merry Christmas, for so many reasons
I'm giving you this gift of love and friendship
You're a special friend and deserve all the love
That comes…
In a Christmas card like this

Step on Back—Snare

Your timing, always just right
I can't resist even with all my might
I'm gonna step back and walk away
I know what you're going to say
You turn on the charm
I'm right back in your arms
I need to step back, my heart crumbles
I want to step back, then I stumble

Step on back
You got me entangled in your snare
I push a little here, I push a little there
Why you keep holding on to me?
Step on back so I can be free.

Step on Back—Today

Today, I'm gonna step back
Step on back and step back again
Today…It's not a question of when.
Today I'm stepping back
I've got to step back, right now, right away
Can't hold on and I can't hold out
I am stepping on back; taking a good long look
If my heart fills with love, I am going to love
Enjoy it, embrace it and set it free
I have got to step back; it is the right thing for me
Right now right away
I can't hold on I can't hold out
I am stepping on back … today

Step on Back—Rx

Let go and love
All that pain that comes with love
Give it up, give it away
It is not about love lost or found
Pain comes from keeping your love bound
Test it, give it up, and give it away
You'll be happy to say
Love isn't love until it is given away

Step on Back—Granny's Panties

Step on back; don't be messin' with granny's panties
Come on, stop makin' fun of Granny
Ain't nothing wrong with granny's panties
They are just right.
They ain't too tight.
Her "bottom" can breathe
And clearly bacteria free.
She don't need disinfectant or a sanitizer.
Granny panties protect her.
Go ahead, Step on back with your silk filled mycoplasma,
Salmonella and dyes
Yeah, you better step on back, Ya' know it aint no lie
Everyone should have a pair or two.
There is a style just for you.
Bikini, low cut and hi-rise
You've never tried them, I must surmise
Go ahead, Step on back, put some sense
In your underwear
Honey, you need air down there!
Step on back, stop messin' with granny, leave her panties alone.
Get down to Wal-Mart; get a pair of you own.
Bloomers, knickers or drawers, call them what you will.
Granny won't let a name distract her from her thrill.
Who cares what "they" say, it's all conjecture.
Granny got it going on. Go ahead, ask her.

Step on back, Step way back, go check it out
Let granny tell you what it is all about.
Step on back, listen to what granny has to say?
She'd get down to it and puts it this way...
It's not the panties or the granny
It is the ...fanny... in the panties
Step on back, Stop trying to speculate
Try on a pair, then you can relate
Bikini, low cut, or hi-rise feels good on the fanny
Step on back and step into some grannies

Chapter 4
Inspiredwordsoul Extra

INSPIREDWORDSOUL DESSERT RECIPE

An enjoyable treat after the main course. Often something sweet
Individual taste should be considered.

Preparation:
A pack of Imagination,
A jar of Visualization
A barrel of Courage
Mix gently a bowl of Sense of humor
with a large cup of laughter
Laughter in the presence of friends
is a good sign of a good relationship

Feelings:
Add for flavor
Slowly simmer: Inspiredwordsoul dessert takes time.
Feel your feelings, you will know when blending is complete.
Add a pinch of emotions, compassion, consideration and caring

Risk:

Sprinkle for zest and firmness, your personal favorites
Add any or all of the following: tears, insanity, love, passion,
conversation or honesty. Mix thoroughly.

Patience:

Reduce heat. You cannot rush Inspiredwordsoul dessert

Sharing:

Share to obtain the satisfactory results, heat at desired
internal temperature. You will be surprised
how much of your heart went into the recipe and
how good you feel because of your efforts.
injury or shock

Caution: Use care in handling. If overly stimulated
with emotions, pause immediately to prevent personal

Happy New Day (Mrs. Sally Womack)

She is giving…loving…and wise
Now take a minute to visualize.
See her setting there, so loving, so caring
…and always sharing
Thoughts like these can soothe the pain.
Like the love in her voice, when she calls your name.
Can you hear …Jackie …Ida …Chinky …Joe …Doris
Sonny …Molly.
How's Pat? How's Dimples? Jackie, it's Sherry
Death brings changes and adjustments for those left behind.
See her setting there? So loving…so kind.
Go ahead, miss her, grieve…feel the pain.
If she were here, she would not complain.
Hear the silence…Feel the love.
That's Mrs. Womack…touching you from above
If she were standing here today
What would you do? What would you say?
"How are you doing" I'd say
And she'd answer;
I'm doing pretty well today;
Happy Birthday, Mrs. Womack…Happy New Day
I missed your Birthday; I'm here to celebrate your New Day.
No more earthly store bought gifts and such.
You have received a greater gift of His tender touch.

We celebrate your journey, as we celebrate your life

No more grief…no more strife.

It was so easy to love you

Everyone, would say, the same thing too.

Ask us, the ones from Seward St, We know so well

Where blood family ended and friends begin, no one could tell

Happy Birthday…Happy New Day

From Sherry, Seward St., Family and friends,

Those who know

You loved them so!

Happy New Day, Mrs. Womack

24 -7 No Time Out For Safety

Robert stepped on a nutting
The nutting moved
Robert is in the hospital
Hoping to improve

Marge pulled a GMPC
Marge stopped
You have probably guessed
The GMPC did not

Rick lifted the GMPC Gate
The safety bar he did not place
Another...light duty case

Safety is 24-7
There is not time out for safety
24 hours 7 days
Robert, Marge and Rick
Did not understand safety pays!

Postal?

Imagine This
A postal worker on Viagra
Coming to work at attention
They really don't need this prescription
No more dragging in with heads down
Ain't got no time to mess around
Punch the clock, get down to business right away
Remember a day's work for a days pay
MDOs bring us to attention
I tell you, we don't need that prescription
For years we have pushed it, pouched it
We've repaired it and patched it and dispatched it
No need for Viagra here
Let me break it down, make it clear
One on one, two on two
Everyone knows who screwing who
One wife today is anothers tomorrow
If you are new in this place
Look, you see a smiley face
These are the facts
Will not be long till you're rammed in the back.
No we don't need Viagra here
There is enough screwing to last for years.

Happy Holiday

It's the day before the Holiday, and all through the station
Not a minute to waste, at least, not in this operation
Mail Processors work with anticipation and care
They cull it, sort it, and tray it.
Mail Handlers are determined, they tractor it,
load it, cancel it. And dispatch it.
Drivers, with care, take the mail on its way
Trucks full of smiles we must deliver today.

Clerks' enthusiasm thrives on getting their work done.
The customer faces make it all fun.
Now because you've paid your dues
Here are some bells for your shoes.
Whenever you are feeling low
Shake your shoes: joy and happiness will flow.
Merry Christmas and Happy New Year
Now go share some Holiday Cheer
Happy Holiday

Postal Christmas Rap

It is 24 - 7 throughout the year
Now it is time for Christmas cheer
Carriers, clerk and mail handlers too,
This Holiday greeting is just for you.

Mechanics, Ets' and Custodians on every tour
I hope you get what you're looking for.
Love, Peace and Happiness to
The EAS and the MVS.

Everyone, Happy Holiday
Enjoy it, your own special way.
It takes a team to do what we do.
That's why this card is just for you!

Happy Holidays

Where are We?

We are here 24-7
It is nowhere near Heaven
We don't make the news
'Till someone decides to pay their dues
Where are we?
It is said we cannot fail
You can't work here if you go to jail
Roller coasters above our heads
Slides above and below our feet
Quality and quantity leaves little time to eat
Where are we?
There are special places to inhale
It gets hot here, no it's not hell
Some say our business won't last forever
Those that work here are much too clever
Where are we?
We work hard this time of year
To bring our customers lots of cheer
Our name is known nationwide
Our drivers are not allowed to
Give anyone a ride

Where are we?
Here it's like a fairy tale
One we know so well
Off to work Grumpy and Sleepy
Once inside, we become Sneezy
And Friday, we're Happy
Where are we?
Look to your left, look to your right
Think about it with all your might
I wrote this poem, don't ask me why
Where are we?
You and I?

No matter what, some days you just don't like your special someone and other days you could not love them more. Everyday is a chance and a challenge to tell them you love them. Here are some quick notes to leave daily every day of the year. Add a little something special on the holidays

Daily "I Love You" Reminders

I value the love you give me and I am so glad you
allow me to share my love with you

You are my friend, you are my joy

Good morning. Have a great day.
I will be thinking of you

Today I offer you love, friendship, respect and freedom

With my total being, I love you

The truth is … I love you more …

Our story of love is not important
What is important is that we are capable of love.

I knew you were the one when I felt as if my heart was trying
to leave my body and I had to get somewhere to kneel and pray

My love for you is perhaps the only glimpse I am permitted of eternity

There was a time I had to leave the room because my emotions
were so intense, now I cannot bear to leave your side.

Your energy is overpowering.
I feel a loss of control whenever you are near

You are everything I have always wanted

If I thank God for putting you in my life
I have to thank Him for the trials that comes with you

I think of our storms as being like the rain and wind
that helps the flowers and plants to grow

Dying does not sadden me as much as the thought of leaving you

We have no control over the past or the future
All we have is now

It means so much to me to look over my shoulder and see you there

The best thing about the beginning of my day and the end of my day,
Is being with you

I am blessed to have you in my life

Sometimes I do not understand you or what it is you're trying to say.
I know whatever it is it is important to us

You have said the words I needed to hear.
They are also the words I have wanted to hear

What would be gained by complaining about yesterday?
Nothing would change. Let us enjoy now

I must ask, are our differences more important than us?

I am sorry if my actions are words cause you to feel
offended or disrespected

Thank you for being in my life

I am blessed I have you to give my love to

For the holidays
I feel the fire works every time I think of you

You are the only gift I need or desire

You are the only gift I want to unwrap this Christmas

I celebrate your birth-day every day

I only know how to love forever

Let me place my hand on your heart. No other
Valentine will do

"You've heard of 3D movies...This is 3D emotions

For ages poetry has been used as an outlet to express the inner affections of the hearts of those in love. While those affections can be hard to describe on paper, Sherry Wright has done it with ease and seems to capture the true human emotions that go along with such passionate sentiments. What initially began as a collection of writings to share with her family and friends soon became an emotional outlet for the attraction author Sherry Wright had towards a special friend. Her compilation of poems became her first-published work entitled Inspired.

Wright wrote each poem as a script, allowing the reader to become the "actor" and feel the range of emotions as they read her heartfelt words. Wright's melodic poems came from what she calls "inspiredwordsoul" which is a mixture of inspiration, imagination and emotions. Although the poems are about relationships, they are not limited to the romantic kind. Many of the poems have a variety of meanings, and Wright leaves it up to the reader to interpret each as they choose.

"I tell people to read' Somethin's in My Water aloud in order to actually feel the message and emotions coming from them," explains Wright. Somethin's in My Water allows the reader to feel...relate, remember, laugh and even love."

Poetry buffs and novices alike can appreciate and connect with the easy-read style of Wright's poems. She effortlessly puts into words the emotions relationships evoke, yet many times are difficult to voice.

About the Author

Sherry Wright has been writing since she was a young child. This is the second book published. She was a commissioned officer in the United States Air Force and spent most of her career in the Military Airlift Command. Sherry attended the University of Nebraska at Omaha Nebraska and has a graduate degree in Urban Studies/Human Resource Planning. She is active in the community and served as a commissioner on the Housing Authority and Judicial Qualification Commission. Her most enjoyable interest are creating and organizing special projects. "My sincere words are easily empathized with by anyone who has felt the joys and sorrows of unconditional love. The poems uniquely describe what so many feel, yet may have a hard time putting into words."